ASCENSION ORACLE

NARI ANASTARSIA

ASCENSION ORACLE

CONNECT TO YOUR SACRED LIGHT

ROCKPOOL

A Rockpool book
PO Box 252
Summer Hill
NSW 2130
Australia

rockpoolpublishing.com

Follow us! **f** © rockpoolpublishing
Tag your images with #rockpoolpublishing

ISBN: 9781922785572

Published in 2023 by Rockpool Publishing
Copyright text and images © Nari Anastarsia, 2023
Copyright design © Rockpool Publishing, 2023

Design by Daniel Poole, Rockpool Publishing
Edited by Brooke Halliwell

Printed and bound in China
10 9 8 7 6 5 4 3 2 1

CONTENTS

I am a traveler you see
I came to this earth to discover
The inner realms of me

I am a traveler you know
Moving through time and space
All things in flow

You are a traveler, you feel it too
The deep call to ascend
Dissolving illusions of you

Candice Godinez

INTRODUCTION

T he overall energy of planet earth is changing, evolving, ascending. Many know this as a time of transitioning from the 3D (3rd dimension) to the 5D (5th dimension).

As vibratory beings of energy, humanity is in a constant dance with the rhythms of the grand cosmic cycles of life. This shift is creating energetic waves that have been affecting humanity physically, mentally and emotionally. It is facilitating accelerated change in the expansion of consciousness. The earth is ascending and so too are we.

To ascend is to raise your vibrational state of consciousness into more expanded states of being. This process of transitioning may not always be easy, as you morph and refine yourself through the energy shifts within you.

The *Ascension Oracle* cards have been divinely created to guide and assist you through this journey of ascension. The energy of this deck will assist you to align your energy with your highest resonance.

For greater understanding of how to better traverse this oracle deck, explore its foundations with the heart-activating *Cosmic Oracle* and be guided by your truth with the next transformational deck, the *Avatar Oracle*. As you move through these oracles consecutively you are better prepared for the wisdom and insights of the *Ascension Oracle*.

This oracle serves as a guide to help strengthen your radiant light and further grow and expand your light body. These cards are inspired by my own journey through this ascension process. I am still unfolding and learning new insights every day that challenge me to greater awareness and understanding of myself. It is an ongoing journey of self-discovery and reflective introspection.

I share these insights through my artworks and messages of this oracle, that you may move through this time of ascension with greater ease. Included also with this deck is information on the chakras, which correspond to the chakra associated with each card message found at the bottom of each page. This section is titled Chakra Tree, as I feel the energy centres within us form an internal energetic tree. A tree that needs to be grounded, supported and nurtured with the freedom to grow. I have also included a Chakra Tree meditation to further nurture your growing light.

Through conscious awareness, understanding and nurturance of your chakras, you can continue to ascend on your evolutionary journey. Information on the chakras can also be found in *Cosmic Oracle* and *Avatar Oracle*. All three decks can be harmoniously used together when doing readings.

Comprised of 36 cards, the *Ascension Oracle* will help you to adjust to the influx of energy streaming in, light waves that are alchemically lifting your frequency in preparation for your next vibrational world of experience.

If you have been drawn to this deck you are part of a group of souls that have been collaboratively dreaming a new world into being. Co-creating heaven on earth through consistent choices of self-love, you radiate light out into the world. Through love, may dualistic perceptions and illusionary layers of untruths be stripped away.

May this oracle assist you to raise your vibration with ease and become the embodiment of love, the truth of who you are. As we move through this time of accelerated expansion of consciousness, keep an open heart and remember your commitment to the light.

It is my intention that the *Ascension Oracle* will help prepare you even more for the next vibrational world of consciousness. May these cards be wisely used to further strengthen your connection to the one infinite creator.

With love and gratitude always

Nari Anastasia

HOW TO USE THE CARDS

T ake a deep breath in and breathe out. Sit quietly and comfortably with the oracle deck in your hands. Feel the energy of gratitude, allowing this energy of gratitude to grow. By feeling grateful, you lift your vibrational frequency and strengthen your connection to source.

Connecting to your heart space, feel the energy of the cards and affirm that it is your intention to use these cards wisely as a tool to connect directly with source energy for guidance and clarity.

– ORACLE PRAYER –

Great Spirit, cleanse my body so that I may be a clear channel of light. Thank you for the clarity and wisdom in interpreting this oracle. Through unconditional love I now invite inspiration to flow to me through these cards. Cleanse these cards of any energy that does not serve my highest good and the good of those I do readings for. May these cards always serve as an instrument of peace, love and spiritual truth. To the source of all creation, I give thanks.

There are different card spreads offered below that you can choose from. Alternatively, you can:

- create your own spread
- shuffle the deck and take the cards that fall out
- lay the cards out and pick the cards that you feel most drawn to.

Do what feels most comfortable for you. Trust your means of connection. As long as your intentions are coming from a space of love, the oracle deck will work for you. You may have a specific question that you wish to say out loud. If you don't have a specific question, you may simply ask for any messages that will best guide you at this moment in your life. If you get repeating cards, pay attention: there is most definitely a message in that for you.

ORACLE CARD SPREADS

ONE-CARD SPREAD
(Message for reflection)

Single card reading that will give you a message that you most need to reflect on for direction and clarity.

- Shuffle the cards.
- Formulate your question.
- Choose **one card**, or select the card that jumps out of the deck.
- Reflect on that message and allow its guidance to be revealed.
- Give thanks.

TWO-CARD SPREAD
(Reflective mirror)

A two-card reading is a wonderful yet simple mini reading
that you can use to gain insight on what is mirrored to you
through your vibrational energy.

- Shuffle the cards.

- Formulate your question – what do I need to see or
  understand more clearly in my life right now?

- Choose **two cards**, or select the cards that jump out of
  the deck.

- **Card one:** the current energy of where you are at.

- **Card two:** what is being mirrored to you.

SIX-CARD SPREAD
(In-depth reading)

The six-card spread offers a more in-depth reading to guide you on your life path. It is a wonderful spread to connect more deeply with your soul.

- Shuffle the cards.
- Choose **six cards**, or select the cards that jump out of the deck.
- Place them in the shape as seen in the diagram.
- **Card one:** current energy – what is happening right now.
- **Card two:** what you need to balance/address or shed.
- **Card three:** what you need to be aware of.
- **Card four:** what you can do to support your growing light.
- **Card five:** what you are moving into.
- **Card six:** overall energy for the whole reading.

THE CHAKRA TREE

 ROOT CHAKRA – earth (red)

The journey through the chakra tree begins at the root chakra located at the base of the spine. This is the foundation of your internal chakra tree. This is where you directly connect to the earth. In order for you to grow, your roots must first trust they are supported by Mother Earth for all their earthly needs. When you can establish that love connection and trust in the earth, there is a deep inner knowing that no matter what, all your earthly needs will be taken care of. When your roots are deep in this source of love, your branches have the capacity to grow to heights that reach dimensions of higher consciousness.

 SACRAL CHAKRA – water (orange)

Now that your roots are grounded and supported it is time to be nurtured. This is where you move into your sacral chakra. Located just below the belly button, this space allows for movement and flow. Space of duality, pleasure and intense emotions, this chakra gives you the opportunity to grow. This is where you really embrace that free-spirited child within. Nurture your inner child with the freedom to grow, through love, joy, creativity, exploration and play.

SOLAR PLEXUS CHAKRA – sun/fire (yellow)

Located above the belly button and under the diaphragm, the solar plexus is the fire of the body. It is this space that ignites you with the fuel/fire to keep moving through the chakras. This is the 'I am' space, the centre for personal power, will and action. It is through the willpower of this chakra that you will find the courage and strength to break through habitual patterns and behaviours. The first step in strengthening and developing your willpower is finding the willingness to make change.

 HEART CHAKRA – air (green)

The heart chakra, the centre of love, is all about love and acceptance for self, about having love and compassion for all aspects of yourself. Keep the heart chakra open. Do not allow your experiences to influence you to build walls. These walls only block your ability to truly branch out and grow. Wisdom lies within this space. For the mind to connect with the wisdom of the heart there must not be any walls of resistance. What makes your heart sing? Follow your heart in all that you do.

 THROAT CHAKRA – ether (blue)

The gateway to the upper chakras, this space is all about communication through sound, self-expression and vibration. It is the space of following and living your truth with integrity. Leading the way by first living the way, this is the chakra where your personal vibrational resonance truly shines through. Follow and live your truth always. Remember the power of the spoken word in your life.

 THIRD EYE CHAKRA – spirit/light (indigo)

The mind of light, the third eye chakra brings you the ability to truly see. See beyond the untruths, beyond the illusions and beyond the veil of this physical density. Located at the centre of the forehead slightly above the brows, this is the space of light. How you perceive the world is dependent on how open this space is to the light of consciousness. Be conscious of how much artificial light you absorb. Get out and drink in the light of the sun and meditate regularly. Raising your vibration through gratitude is a wonderful way to activate this chakra.

 CROWN CHAKRA – spirit/thought (gold, purple/pink, white)

Connecting you to the divine source of all life, the crown chakra is all about oneness. It is the space where you truly understand that all is indeed one. Through this understanding there is greater love and compassion for all those around you. You come to understand that every soul is simply beautiful gradients of reflected light, the one creative source of light in which we are all connected.

THE CHAKRA TREE MEDITATION

Gently close your eyes. Take a deep breath in and breathe out. Feel all the tension in your body release. Feeling relaxed, bring your awareness to the soles of your feet.

Feel the energy buzzing in both your feet. Now imagine energetic roots moving out of your feet and into the earth, and see these roots expanding out far and wide. Feel your roots connecting to the heart of Mother Earth. As you meld with the earth, feel yourself becoming one with it. See and feel the colour red.

> Rest in this space for a moment. Feeling oneness
> with the earth, know that you are supported.
> Your roots are deeply grounded in love.

Now feel Mother Earth's nourishing energy travel up your roots and through the soles of your feet. Allow this beautiful energy to move up your body and fill it with so much love. Feel this love nurturing every aspect of you. Feel this warm, tender, loving energy flow throughout your whole body. See and feel the colour orange.

> Rest in this space for a moment. Know that
> you are loved and nurtured always.

Feeling so relaxed and so loved, sense this energy grow within you like the light of the sun. Allow this light to radiate throughout your whole body. Feel yourself growing in strength and power. You are limitless. You are powerful beyond measure. See and feel the colour yellow.

> Rest in this space for a moment. Know that you
> are whole and healthy. You are connected to
> an infinite source of energy for all your needs.

Now bring your awareness to your heart space. Feel this space. Visualise a flower with its petals fully open. See the loving energy flowing through your body enter this flower with so much love. Allow that energy to flood your heart flower with compassion and unconditional love. See and feel the colour green.

> Rest in this space for a moment. Feeling this loving energy, know that you are unconditionally loved and accepted.

As you sit in this space of absolute love, see and feel a radiant blue light shimmering within you. This is the light of truth: your truth. This light encourages you to authentically follow your truth and shine your unique light. Allow this healing light to fill your entire being.

> Rest in this space for a moment. Feeling this blue light throughout your body, know that you are a beautiful healing light to the world. You inspire through your own fearless radiant light.

Bring your awareness now to your forehead, to your third eye. Visualise light growing brighter and brighter in this area. You may feel a tingly vibration in this space; embrace this sensation with love. Allow every cell in your body to be filled with this luminous light, the light of conscious awareness. Remember who you are: you are the light. See and feel the colour indigo.

> Rest in this space for a moment. Through this light of awareness you have the capacity to see through any illusions. You see the deeper truth.

Bathing in this light of consciousness, visualise a flower at the top of your head. See this flower open up fully to the universe and allow the energy of the divine to enter this space. Like warm golden honey, allow this most beautiful energy to fill your entire being. Feel the euphoria and joy flooding your body. Feel this bliss. See and feel the colour violet/pink.

> Rest in this space for a moment. Know that you are so loved. You are connected to the entire constellation of life. You are a divine spark of the one. Sit in this space and bathe in this rapturous feeling of absolute love.

Take in a deep breath and breathe out. Feeling refreshed, energised and completely renewed, bring your awareness back to your body. Wriggle your toes and fingers. Bring your awareness back into your room. When you are ready you may open your eyes.

THE
ORACLE
CARDS

BREATHE

'BREATH IS THE BRIDGE WHICH CONNECTS
LIFE TO CONSCIOUSNESS, WHICH UNITES
YOUR BODY TO YOUR THOUGHTS.'
– THICH NHAT HANH

If you have been drawn to this card, stay conscious
of your breathing patterns. Through breath you are
able to take in energy, calm the mind, balance the
emotions, relax and unwind.

Oxygen contains light particles that nourish the
mind, body and spirit. It is the divine breath that
gives life to all of creation, filling our bodies with
sacred life force energy.

Bring your awareness back to breath. Is it deep
or shallow? Is your energy constricted by emotional

charges? The emotional state is very much influenced through breath and vice-versa. By consciously being aware of your breath and taking the time to practise conscious breathing, you can help your body clear the channels of emotional blocks. This will open you up for healing and energetic nourishment.

Conscious breathing amplifies life-force energy and helps maintain your natural high-vibrational state despite whatever situation or environment you find yourself in. The breath is the connecting force between mind and body. Through natural conscious breathing you will find yourself more present and inspired with the riches and wonders of life.

EXERCISE Bring your attention to your breath. Take a deep breath in, expand your belly then your chest. Now exhale and release any tension. Repeat this technique throughout the day.

AFFIRMATION I am replenished and restored through the breath of life.

CHANGE

**TRUST THE CHANGE IN CURRENTS;
IT IS TAKING YOU ON A JOURNEY
INTO SELF-REALISATION.**

If you have drawn this card you may be moving through waves of change in your life. Change is inevitable.

Stay balanced and remain flexible as you navigate your way through powerful waters of the soul. When you are resistant and do not allow your soul to flow with the moving currents, tension is imposed on your body. Energy blocks are formed and your soul is held back from its evolutionary journey into expanded consciousness.

It is all too easy to stay with what is comfortable, with old habits and patterns, but your soul yearns for more. Release all fears, doubts and concerns. Trust in the universal river of life, for it carries your soul to environments and situations that best allow your soul to grow.

You are supported, loved one, so let go and allow your life to be guided with love. When you do this with complete trust and faith, you allow your highest self to complete the mission it came here to do: co-create a joy-filled life, blessed with love.

Trust that this intelligent universal source of love is guiding you always.

EXERCISE Say out loud: 'I am open to change and trust that I am guided by love.'

AFFIRMATION I surrender to the universal river of life, and trust that no matter what I will always come out on top.

ASCENDING SOUL

RISE UP AND BE THE LIGHT
THAT SHINES THE WAY.

You are the embodiment of love; this is your true self. This creative light and power continue to reveal themselves more each day.

There may be moments, however, when this light is overshadowed by the cloudy waters of your emotions and you feel as though you are becoming unhinged. Loved one, the old paradigm within you, with all its limitations, is falling away. Light waves from the sun are being emitted, transforming and preparing your body for your next evolutionary chapter.

Be patient. Every challenge, be it physical, mental or emotional, is simply layers of limiting beliefs being shifted. If you are feeling overwhelmed, remember: your magnificent light is unfolding and everything you are going through is the unfoldment of absolute love.

You are ascending and elevating your vibration to a more expanded state of being. Through this transformation, the magnificence of your loving presence will assist others on their journey back into the light of love.

Remember, the more you love the faster you vibrate.

EXERCISE Close your eyes and relax. Visualise a beautiful light glowing at your heart centre. See this light growing and expanding. Feel this light growing stronger and more radiant. Feeling completely at peace and in harmony with all, be one with this light. Remember always that you are the light.

AFFIRMATION I let go of what no longer serves me, and with strength, courage and faith I open myself up to the light of love that I truly am.

WHOLENESS

'ALL HEALING IS ESSENTIALLY THE RELEASE FROM FEAR.'

– A COURSE IN MIRACLES

There are times in your life you feel tested by the challenges of the human body. Human frailties and vulnerabilities can test and challenge your mind into believing that you are not strong, whole or powerful.

Stay conscious, loved one; the ego can sometimes work through your denser body to conspire against your mind. It is only when you are in two minds that disempowerment occurs. Do not allow your body to be a mirror of a split mind. This is conflicting energies in your mind that may have you feeling doubtful and disconnected from your divinity.

Return your mind back to the unified presence of spirit, of oneness and wholeness.

By staying strong and firm in this belief of wholeness your body will entrain to this vibration and naturally return to its whole, balanced and healthy state. When you trust in spirit and remember your divine light, miracles are imminent.

Allow your mind to merge into the oneness of our infinite creator and regain authentic limitless power. Allow your mind, loved one, to return into the wholeness of love.

EXERCISE Close your eyes. Take a deep breath in and breathe out. Visualise a shimmering light between your brows where the third eye is located. See this light growing, expanding out through your whole body. Repeat: 'I am of one mind with our infinite creator.'

AFFIRMATION I am whole, balanced and healthy. I am empowered with strength, as I remember my oneness with source.

PRESENCE

'WHEN YOU LOVE SOMEONE, THE
BEST THING YOU CAN OFFER IS
YOUR PRESENCE. HOW CAN YOU
LOVE, IF YOU ARE NOT THERE?'

– THICH NHAT HANH

The key to reining in your busy mind from its scattered wanderings from past to future is focusing your attention on the present moment.

When you return your conscious awareness and attention to the here and now you liberate your mind and find peace in the stillness of presence.

Apprehension may stem from thoughts about the future, while old wounds may anchor you to the memories of the past. Do not allow your mind to draw your attention away from this very moment.

Should you catch your mind wondering aimlessly, take a deep breath and bring your attention to the here and now. Allow your feet to ground you to the present moment, like a deep-rooted tree. When your roots are planted firmly in the here and now you stand strong. The light of who you are will then shine at its brightest. In turn this radiant light attracts blessings of love in its many forms.

Just by being present you free yourself from unnecessary internal suffering and life becomes simpler. When you see each moment as a gift of love your life is immensely enriched with blessings of prosperity and joy.

Free yourself with the powerful presence of love.

EXERCISE Go for a walk.
Pay attention to your steps.
Feel your breath flowing in and out.
Be present.

AFFIRMATION I am here; the time is now.

INNER POWER

'IF WE WISH TO ASCEND THE MOUNTAIN
PATH OF THE WARRIOR, WE NEED
TO FACE THE HURDLES TO SELF-
MASTERY THAT LIE IN OUR PATH.'

– DAN MILLMAN

Within you there is an abundant wellspring of great strength and unlimited power. This card serves as a reminder of that power. Look closely at your life and see where you may possibly be giving away some of your power.

Loss of power can come from attachments, addictions or any situation that may have you controlled by external forces and circumstances.

Is there any part of your life you may be slave to instead of master?

Stay conscious of the polarities within you. Review your life and apply your force of will to the transition back into the wholeness of power. You have what it takes to rise above any seemingly difficult situation.

Remember who you are – you are the light of the divine. Through the nurturing of this light the areas within your mind that serve to disempower will be no more. You hold the key to change. The divine light within you is indeed real and will assist you to transmute any energy that keeps you from being the powerful creator that you are.

EXERCISE Focus on strengthening an area in your life that could benefit from more balance. It could be as simple as making the decision to sleep earlier, stretch, walk daily or replace an habitual pattern for something that nurtures your mind, body and soul.

AFFIRMATION I am an empowered being of light connected through love to the universal source of oneness.

7

VULNERABILITY
IS POWER

**BEING VULNERABLE ALLOWS THE BEAUTY
OF YOUR SOUL TO TRULY SHINE.**

Vulnerability is so often seen as being weak. In truth,
your ability to truly express your emotions and
deepest feelings are great indicators of your level of
courage and strength.

Loved one, it is so easy to wear masks and
hide behind walls of strength, but when you open
yourself up to the truth of how you feel you enrich
your life and align to the highest version of yourself.

When you are vulnerable you are choosing to live a wholehearted experience. It is living courageously from a place of authenticity.

Have you been allowing yourself to be truly vulnerable? Life is all about growing and expanding. When you are vulnerable you live an empowered life. This empowerment comes from the acceptance of self rather than needing to be accepted by others. It is honouring your truth without the fear of being judged by another.

Liberate yourself by expressing what is in your heart and allow yourself to be truly seen. As you do this you unfold even more to the light of love that is truly you.

EXERCISE Reflect on your life. Are there times when you wear armour to protect yourself from being vulnerable?

AFFIRMATION I allow myself to be truly seen through the authentic expression of my divine soul.

8

FOUNDATIONS

'LOVE SHOULD BE A TREE WHOSE ROOTS ARE DEEP IN THE EARTH, BUT WHOSE BRANCHES EXTEND INTO HEAVEN.'
– BERTRAND RUSSELL

Through the collective shift in consciousness, there may be many moments of feeling anxious. Uncertainty around stability, safety, health, family and finances can be overwhelming.

Loved one, if your sense of groundedness is being shaken by the external, with all that is taking place in the world, it is time to look deeper at where your sense of groundedness and stability stems.

Spiritual grounding is being firmly rooted in knowing you are never alone. You are one with source.

Through this connectivity and oneness you are always supported and looked after. It is a knowing that despite what is happening in your outer reality, you are always safe: safe to feel and experience everything that comes up for you.

When you are in alignment with this truth you are empowered with the strength, resilience and clarity to flourish. You have the capacity to grow to infinite heights with the knowing that your foundations are built on the solid grounds of love, faith and trust.

> **EXERCISE** Take your shoes off and stand on the earth. Visualise roots of light moving through your feet connecting to the earth. Allow any excess energy from the tensions of everyday life to move out of your body and into the earth to be neutralised.

> **AFFIRMATION** I am safe to feel and experience all of life.

9

HEART FLOWER

**'HOW YOU LOVE YOURSELF IS HOW
YOU TEACH OTHERS TO LOVE YOU.'**

– RUPI KAUR

This card comes to you as a gentle reminder to look at the relationship you have with yourself. Are you embracing every aspect of yourself with unconditional love, compassion and acceptance?

Loved one, it is time to take others off that pedestal and turn your attention on the unique light of love that is you. When you can accept, love and embrace the magnificence of your soul your external relationships will come to mirror that level of love.

Observe any negative self-talk that may come up as you nurture your heart flower with absolute love.

Enter that space of love within your own heart and allow it to blossom. When you do this you attract relationships that resonate and reflect your increased levels of love.

When you return to love within yourself you awaken to the unity of the one heart. Feeling the ecstasy and frequency of unity consciousness, you bathe in the full glory and remembrance of being.

As your heart flower blooms you experience the resonance and expansive joy of the one universal heartbeat.

EXERCISE Look at your reflection in the mirror and repeat: 'I love you, I accept you, you are beautiful, you are amazing, you are worthy of love, because you are love.'

AFFIRMATION I accept and unconditionally love every facet of myself.

10

EARTH ANGEL

'HUMANS BECOME ANGELS ON EARTH, NOT IN HEAVEN.'

– PARAMAHANSA YOGANANDA

Thank you for being you. Your light is magnificent and ever so bright. The gift of heaven's wings is yours.

Earth angel, you are so loved and supported on your journey. Everything you have gone through and things you may still be going through have been guiding you to fly.

Do not doubt your ability to assist humanity. These beliefs serve nothing other than to slow your progress. Through the divine expression of your creative soul you are a channel of healing light to the world.

You are unique, and what you have to offer humanity is a gift of pure love. The universe has your back, earth angel and rejoices in your authentic expression of creative light. Allow this creative fire to ignite new ideas that will light the way into your next exciting chapter. Thank you for courageously shining your light and inspiring others to their own inner truth.

Love in its many spectrums of colour surround you; embrace this time and cherish every moment. You are in alignment with your highest self. Take time to celebrate your life and go forward with increased light and power.

EXERCISE Create an artwork of your divine soul. Create this piece with no judgement, criticism or limiting beliefs.

AFFIRMATION I am love made visible.

11

MIND GARDEN

SOW SEEDS OF LOVE IN THE GARDEN OF YOUR MIND AND HEAVEN ON EARTH WILL BE REALISED.

Your mind is your garden and the seeds planted there are your thoughts. Seeds that are watered are thoughts that consistently play in your mind. These thoughts eventually come into fruition.

It can be easy to fall unconscious to inner dialogue and thought patterns. Loved one, your soul is advancing and your vibration is being raised. To help with this evolutionary journey, stay conscious of your thoughts. Cultivate only seeds in your mind garden that you truly wish to grow.

Now is the time to tend to the garden of your mind. Water only seeds of love with complete faith and trust. When you do this your inner garden becomes your sanctuary and you a true master.

When heaven becomes your natural state of mind the chaos of the holographic world ceases to disrupt your inner peace. You come to see life as a grand cosmic play that transforms and awakens souls.

Within you there is a deep knowing that all will be played out victoriously.

> **EXERCISE** Take time out throughout the day to observe your thoughts and inner dialogue. Are your thoughts in alignment with your highest resonance?

> **AFFIRMATION** I am nurturing the inner garden of my mind with unconditional love and compassion.

12

RETURN TO INNOCENCE

**RETURNING TO INNOCENCE IS
MOVING BACK INTO THE ONENESS
OF LOVE WITHIN YOU.**

This oracle asks you to open up more to the divine child within you, to explore life with an open heart and open mind.

Life need not be so serious. Bring humour into the exploration of yourself and the world around you. Consciously make time to have fun and feel alive through spontaneous play and laughter.

What brings you joy? What makes your heart sing? Move back into that space of wonderment and allow your heart to be nurtured by the miracles of love all around you. See and feel the luminosity of a single flower. Feel the energising hug from the grounding presence of a deep-rooted tree.

When you nurture your inner child with love there is a return to innocence. You remember your divinity and move back into an expanded state of being.

Loved one, it is time to truly open yourself up to the magic of life by aligning yourself with what brings you joy. Lighten up by embodying your inner child with the simple presence of unconditional love.

> **EXERCISE** Bring more humour into your daily life. Blow bubbles, play hide and seek, draw, sing, play, explore and dance in the rain.

> **AFFIRMATION** I am a divine child of the universe.

13

REST

'BE GENTLE WITH YOURSELF AS YOU HONOUR THE NATURAL EBBS AND FLOW OF ASCENSION.'

– NARAYNE

If you have drawn this card you are being asked to surrender fully to the restorative power of rest. Through rest you will be able to attune and assimilate to the intense energies moving through you.

Loved one, allow yourself to just be. Let go without judgement or resistance and simply rest in love. By allowing yourself to slow down through this time of accelerated energy you are better able to digest and recalibrate your own frequency.

There may be times, however, when you feel you should be doing more. This oracle reminds you to honour the process of transformation. Release any guilt or shame that may arise from taking time out for you and move into your own rhythms and cycles of rest.

Trust that you can take time out to replenish, restore and attune without being consumed by the solidarity of your journey. As you step away from an outmoded frequency of reality you reconnect with yourself in a more powerful way.

EXERCISE Take time out to simply rest. Replenish your body with self-care and love.

AFFIRMATION I honour my soul by taking time out to rest.

FREEDOM

'IT'S EASY TO STAND IN THE CROWD BUT IT TAKES COURAGE TO STAND ALONE.'

– MAHATMA GANDHI

In this changing world you are constantly faced with choices, making decisions based on the external general consensus or aligning yourself with your inner wisdom and truth.

It is so easy to feel as though you don't fit in, to feel as though you don't belong when making choices that are guided by your heart.

Loved one, you are so unique and your light is radiant. Do not for one second dim down your magnificent light to fit into a paradigm of what is perceived as the norm. Be that catalyst for change by staying true to you.

Surrender yourself completely to your creative passions and lose yourself entirely to the freedom of your own song. You honour yourself by living from the heart more deeply. Through your courage you inspire those around you to live a more authentic, free-spirited life.

Boldly stand in your light and co-create a greater world through love. Anchor in the light by always following your own heart and truth.

> **EXERCISE** Say out loud: 'I look within for the answers I seek and perceive its wisdom through unconditional love.'

> **AFFIRMATION** I am guided by the light of truth within me always.

EMPOWERMENT

'FEELING THE ONENESS OF YOURSELF WITH ALL THINGS IS TRUE LOVE.'
– ECKHART TOLLE

True power comes not from the external. Instead, it is sourced from your direct ability to connect to the divine within you. When your source of power is coming from your internal connection to the infinite, all illusions of separation are disintegrated.

When you draw on the wisdom and power from this source of oneness your actions and choices are aligned with integrity and truth. You become a clear instrument of light and a living embodiment of love.

Through this source of empowerment you strengthen your light body and attune yourself to the vibration of love. No longer do you live your life through the cloudiness of the human lens; instead, you live from a place of clarity, a space beyond the polarities and illusions of duality.

Loved one, merge entirely into this space of oneness. Attune your frequencies to this universal source for harmony in all areas of your life.

EXERCISE Take time out to meditate. Connect to your inner light and power. Amplify this energy through gratitude.

AFFIRMATION I am empowered through the knowing; I am one with the divine source of love.

NEW CYCLE

'LIFE IS LIKE RIDING A BICYCLE. TO KEEP YOUR BALANCE, YOU MUST KEEP MOVING.'
– ALBERT EINSTEIN

This card brings forth a period of resurrection and restoration. The darker period of your life is now coming to an end and a new cycle begins. The flowers of your soul have begun to bloom. With an open heart, be ready to receive.

This new cycle heralds exciting opportunities, prosperity and bliss. Your soil is fertile, loved one, so any ideas that are planted during this time will come into fruition, blessed with abundance and love.

You have been gifted many golden treasures born from adversity and challenges and now carry gems of radiant light within you. Use this time to shine your much-expanded light.

Feel the excitement, joy and inspiration growing inside you and be ready, for the best is yet to come.

> **EXERCISE** Your ability to manifest is strong. Use this time to visualise whatever it is you would like to bring into being. Feel joy and gratitude as though you are already living the visualised dream.

> **AFFIRMATION** Trusting in the cycles of life, I confidently move forward with expanded light.

DIVINE PLAN

TRUST IN THE DIVINE PLAN. YOU ARE BEING GUIDED IN THE DIRECTION THAT WILL BEST ALLOW YOUR SOUL TO GROW.

Trust in the divine plan that is beautifully unfolding in your life right now. Do not allow doubts, fears and a lack of trust to hold you back from moving forward into the unknown.

Loved one, you do not need to know how everything will work out or have a step-by-step guide to predict what lies ahead. You are being guided in the direction that will best allow your soul to grow. Staying where you are will only cause stagnation and dissatisfaction. Release all fears, for this chapter is bringing you lessons of faith and trust.

Will you embrace these gifts of love and allow your soul to move forward fearlessly, or will you resist the seasons of change? To resist is to stay in a space of complacency, comfortability and fear.

You may not fully understand what is taking place in your life right now, but rest assured it is for your own growth. Trust and have faith in the divine plan that is at work in your life. A more empowered life awaits on the other side of discomfort and fear.

EXERCISE Visit an ocean, lake or river. Go into the water and allow yourself to gently float and energetically meld with the moving tides. Feel the natural flow of the moving currents.

AFFIRMATION I trust that I am being guided to the full expression of my divine soul.

UNFOLDING LIGHT

WHEN THE ILLUSIONS OF IDENTITY AND SELF FALL AWAY THE TRUTH OF WHO WE ARE IS REVEALED.

Right now you are going through a time of transition. All that is inauthentic and not aligned with your highest self is breaking down. You are returning into the fullness and wholeness of being.

As hard as this period may be, have faith and allow this process to unfold. There is no need to try to keep it together or control the natural evolution of your soul. Think of this time as an opportunity to transcend and release all that has been holding you back.

Surrender. Have faith and trust in what is taking place. Use this time to practise self-love and remember the universe is not against you or punishing you in any way. The old is simply falling away. As the facade of what limits and defines you falls away your true radiance and magnificence shine through.

EXERCISE Breathing gently, place your hands on your heart and repeat the following mantra: 'I surrender with faith and trust to the light of love unfolding within me.' Visualise this light growing inside you, expanding out all around you.

AFFIRMATION I release all that does not serve my highest self as I unfold to the illuminating light of love that I am.

TRANSMUTATION

**WHERE YOUR ATTENTION
GOES, ENERGY FLOWS.**

If you have picked this card you may be feeling the intense energies of transmutation. The physical and emotional intensity from these energies can be very overwhelming, and there may be many moments of feeling off balance as your body attunes to the incoming frequencies of light.

Loved one, you are in the process of alchemical transmutation. Your body is being adjusted for the final quantum leap through light. These energetic adjustments have been preparing and crafting your light body for the final ascension into your next vibrational world of experience.

You may feel this change on a deeper conscious level. A knowing that what is taking place is part of this transformational process. Allow yourself to move through this time with no judgement. Denying or resisting this process may amplify or prolong the intensity of your experience.

Allow your heart to guide you. To move through this chapter with greater ease is to integrate the dualities within. Embrace shadow aspects of self with love. Through this integration you are liberated from the defining polarities of good versus evil, light versus dark and right versus wrong.

Embrace this time and see it as a wonderful opportunity to expand into the full essence of being.

EXERCISE Close your eyes and breathe gently in and out. Bring your awareness to your body. Now bring your awareness to every cell in your body. With unconditional love, visualise and feel a beautiful healing white light growing within the heart of every cell.

AFFIRMATION I embrace and integrate the shadow aspects of myself with unconditional love.

20

CONSCIOUS CREATOR

**FREE YOURSELF FROM THE
LIMITATIONS OF YOUR MIND BY
SHINING THE LIGHT OF AWARENESS
ON THE POWER OF YOUR BELIEFS.**

Loved one, you already understand the power of
beliefs and the role it plays in shaping and mirroring
the entire constellation of your life.

You have the wisdom of knowing which beliefs
serve to empower and disempower. Now is the time
to reflect on the strength and power of each belief
you hold within you despite it being detrimental
or beneficial.

Take an honest look within and determine the
energy you have been giving to each belief. Through a

simple observation of these beliefs you will better understand yourself and the world around you. You have the power to turn the volume of energy down on beliefs that do not serve you and increase the energy towards beliefs that empower you.

This step is crucial when moving into self-mastery of conscious creation. When you are completely conscious of your own energetic make-up you can truly live the life you were born to live.

Through complete awareness you are liberated from the illusions of your mind and remember in totality your oneness with the infinite source of all that is.

EXERCISE On a piece of paper, list different topics and write down your beliefs on each. Next to each belief rate the strength of that belief. For example, Topic – love. Belief – I am lovable. Strength of belief – 7.5/10. Examine your notes. Strengthen the beliefs that empower.

AFFIRMATION I consciously choose empowering beliefs to shape my reality.

21

NURTURE

**TRUST IN THE DIVINE FOR THE
NURTURANCE OF YOUR SOUL.**

Within you there is an internal wellspring of love, an infinite reservoir of sustenance to nourish your soul.

Loved one, this card encourages you to remember your oneness with this source of love. When you trust in this connection your soul is continuously nourished with absolute love.

Integrate this knowing in your everyday life through acts of self-love, and always will your cup be full. By embracing this truth in oneness you will always know your worth. You are a spark of the divine, a magnificent being of light, love in human form.

Through this knowing and wholeness of being you draw to you souls who can meet you as you authentically are, souls who are also nourished by the source of eternal love.

Open yourself up more fully to the rapture and richness of this cornucopia of love. You are so very loved and nurtured always.

EXERCISE Take some time out to self-nurture. What brings you joy? Perhaps a long bath, a walk at the beach, a day of pampering and a massage.

AFFIRMATION I trust that I am nurtured always by the divine source of love.

INTENTION

WHEN YOUR INTENTION COMES FROM A PLACE OF TRUTH AND AUTHENTICITY, DOORS OF OPPORTUNITIES NATURALLY OPEN.

Intention is so much more than having a strong will and focused determination. Intention is a powerful universal force that holds infinite potential energy. This power is accessible to you, loved one.

Now is the time to plant seeds of intention towards your desired dream or vision. Use this power of intention to naturally harness the magic that surrounds you. This omnipresent force will guide and carry you in the direction of your dreams, dreams that are aligned with your highest self.

There are no limits. Let this next chapter be filled with miraculous experiences that transcend any limitations that you may hold. When you harness this powerful force from a place of truth and authenticity you are always supported.

Be specific when tapping into this power of intention to bring forth your wishes and envision your desired outcome with gratitude. Celebrate this power and embrace this guiding force in all aspects of your life.

EXERCISE Think about your goals and write them down. Next to each goal, write down your intentions. For example, Goal – financial freedom. Intention – so that I may spend more time with friends and family.

AFFIRMATION The seeds of my creative thoughts naturally blossom through the nurturance of love.

DIVINE UNION

BALANCE IS THE BLENDING OF THE DIVINE MASCULINE AND FEMININE ENERGY WITHIN.

The divine feminine and the divine masculine are sacred polarities that exist in all life. This card comes to you so that you can explore the play of these polarities within yourself for inner union.

When the masculine and feminine energies are not unified within you there is an ongoing search in the external world for that missing aspect from your energy, be it the masculine looking for balance with the feminine in the external or vice-versa. There is a subconscious attraction to those of the opposite energy for that feeling of fulfilment.

When you balance and unify these inner polarities you no longer need relationships to complete you. Through this union within yourself there is wholeness in love. There is no neediness or attachment; there is simply a sharing of divine love.

That search for equilibrium with another to fill any void or loneliness is replaced by the fullness and richness of being. Through this unification there is internal harmony. Loved one, your external experiences and relationships will come to mirror your internal balance.

EXERCISE Reflect on your internal relationship. Do you resonate with having more masculine or feminine energy? If uncertain, do some research on the qualities each part holds. Now visualise with love both parts coming together as one within you.

AFFIRMATION I unite the divine masculine and feminine within me through unconditional love.

NEW BEGINNINGS

'WHEN ONE DOOR CLOSES, ANOTHER OPENS.'
– ALEXANDER GRAHAM BELL

This card signals a breakthrough in your life. Doors that were once closed are now open. Now is the time to walk through those doors with courage, strength and trust.

Do not allow self-doubt and fears to stop you from moving forward. Continuously trust and follow the stirrings of your heart. You are being guided in the direction of your dreams.

Give thanks to the many lessons that you have moved through and embrace the memories of your past. Take a deep breath and release that which no longer serves you. Allow your next wonderful adventure to unfold.

Wonderful opportunities are in store for you: new beginnings, new perceptions and new connections. You have so much to offer and will see this more as you courageously move forward.

Your light is radiant, loved one. You are being guided to places and environments that will encourage and support your growing light. Make way to experience a more expanded way of being.

EXERCISE Say this declaration: 'I release all that does not serve me and choose to move forward to environments that nourish my soul to grow.'

AFFIRMATION I release and let go all that does not serve my true authentic self and move forward with faith, trust and courage.

25

SUPPORT

WE ARE SUPPORTED WHEN OUR FOUNDATIONS ARE BUILT ON THE FULL REALISATION THAT WE ARE ONE.

This card serves to remind you that you are never alone. You are ethereally surrounded and supported by beings of light, connected to the one heart.

Sometimes there may be feelings of not being supported. Loved one, release any beliefs you may hold of separation. You are one with source. Know this truth.

When you follow your heart you are in alignment with your highest self, the self that is connected to the oneness of life. When you connect to this divine support system of the universe, like a spiral effect that energy of support expresses itself to you through loving beings aligned to your vibrational state of oneness. All illusions that come from feeling separate from the whole are lost when you remember your oneness with all that is.

Keep going, loved one, and be open to receiving support at a whole new level. The light of love is pouring forth the strength, energy, patience and peace needed for you right now. Move forward with the wisdom that the creator has your back.

EXERCISE Place your hands on your heart and feel gratitude in knowing that you are supported always. Your guides and angels are always around you.

AFFIRMATION I have faith and trust that I am supported and guided always.

26

LOVE UNCONDITIONALLY

'WHEN YOU JUDGE ANOTHER, YOU DO NOT DEFINE THEM, YOU DEFINE YOURSELF.'

– WAYNE DYER

The more you remember your wholeness and oneness with the divine the greater your capacity to love.

Through this illumination you are better able to see the polarities between light and dark within yourself and others. There is greater love and acceptance for yourself and those around you. There is no judgement, competition or control through spiritual hierarchy. Instead, there is a knowing and understanding that all is playing out as it should and all souls are simply playing their roles at different stages of their evolutionary journey.

Loved one, you understand this truth. You have deepened your connection to the realisation we are all one, the realisation that your feelings towards others are simply reflections of yourself.

Use this wisdom and shine your light to the world. Radiate your unconditional love, acceptance and compassion in all areas of your life. Allow this light to be magnified through the full presence of being.

Through this unconditional love you birth a new world into creation.

EXERCISE Feel unconditional love, acceptance and compassion within you. Allow that loving vibration to radiate out to the rest of the world.

AFFIRMATION I am, we are.

27

INFINITE ABUNDANCE

**'ABUNDANCE IS NOT SOMETHING WE
ACQUIRE; IT IS SOMETHING WE TUNE INTO.'**

– WAYNE DYER

You are being invited to step into your power and connect more fully to the infinite abundance all around you. It is time to stop playing it small and embrace your part in the co-creative dance of creation.

Release limiting beliefs that stop you from truly opening up to the generous infinite blessings of abundance. Take off the cap in your ability to manifest abundance on all levels of being.

Spirit is beckoning you to realise your greatness. By clearing the blocks that limit your soul you open up to the infinite field of possibilities. The ability to manifest on a larger scale becomes effortless and natural.

As limiting beliefs fall away you connect more deeply to life's guiding light. Through this light you are propelled naturally and organically to abundance, blessings and prosperity in all areas of your life. With a deep feeling of gratitude, watch as blessings unfold.

EXERCISE Close your eyes. Visualise a wall with many bricks. Each brick symbolises a belief or block that keeps you from truly opening up to abundance. Place your hands on that wall and send this wall absolute love and compassion. As you do this, allow this wall to melt away. As it melts, see a golden door. Go through that door and visualise golden light of abundance, prosperity and love raining down on you. Allow yourself to completely merge with this golden light of love.

AFFIRMATION I am infinite and limitless, abundantly blessed in all areas of my life.

28

TRANSITIONING WORLDS

'DO NOT CONFORM TO THE PATTERN OF THIS WORLD, BUT BE TRANSFORMED BY THE RENEWING OF YOUR MIND.'

– ROMANS 12:2

During this time of transitioning into a new vibrational paradigm there may be many moments you feel disillusioned by what is real. You may find yourself reassessing what it is you truly value and disconnecting from the material plane fields and defining constructs of this reality.

Loved one, you are not alone, although there may be many moments you feel isolated as people around you may not comprehend your change. You might find yourself disengaged by the world around you and find inner solace in retreating to your inner sanctum of peace.

Trust the process. All is unfolding as it should. You are in perfect harmony and resonance with the grand cosmic design that is at play.

Loved one, you are currently walking between two worlds: the world of duality and the world of unity and oneness. As you shift back and forth in consciousness from an old way of being to the new you, stay conscious of your choices. Are your choices coming from a place of love or fear?

The more you embrace your divine light the easier this shift will be. You will be able to not only live in this world but thrive without the constrains of its dualistic nature.

EXERCISE Spend more time connecting to the heart of the earth; for example, bushwalks, gardening and so on. Through her loving presence, she will ground you through this time of change.

AFFIRMATION I am expanding my light through conscious choices of self-love.

29

REFLECTIVE MIRRORS

'YOUR LIFE IS A MIRROR. LIFE GIVES US NOT WHAT WE WANT. LIFE GIVES US WHO WE ARE.'

– ROBIN S. SHARMA

There are opportunities to better know yourself through the many mirrors of self-reflection. Pay attention to the different mirrors around you. What do they help you see within yourself? Do you hold judgement or resentment or perhaps get emotionally charged by the experiences of some of the mirrors around you?

What shadows are these mirrors bringing up? Mirrors can reveal the parts within that are in most need of compassion and love. These hidden parts most often stay locked in the deepest recesses of self. Through acceptance and self-love, this energy can be transmuted into light.

As challenging as some mirrors can be, see each reflective experience as a wonderful opportunity to grow. With greater awareness and clarity, watch as your world slowly transforms into heaven on earth.

By viewing each mirror with gratitude and love, every experience becomes beautiful reflections of light.

EXERCISE Pay attention to what triggers you. What energies are being brought to the surface? Is there a pattern? When did you first feel this emotional trigger? Go back to that moment and send unconditional love and compassion to the part of you that was hurt.

AFFIRMATION I am grateful for the opportunity to grow through the reflective mirrors around me.

30

ASCENSION SYMPTOMS

'THE MORE BALANCED THE BODY, THE MORE EASILY WE CAN FEEL THE UPLIFTING PRESENCE OF SPIRIT.'

– DAN MILLMAN

If you have picked this card you are on the optimal timeline of ascension. Be patient and gentle with your body during this time.

As light particles flow in through solar waves and hit the densities within the body, discomfort may be felt. The denser energy within may have difficulty interacting with the light. This may be felt physically, mentally and emotionally.

Loved one, as challenging and confusing as this period may be, the universe is actually supporting you to shift all that does not serve you. This dense energy is made up of deep-rooted fears and limitations that keep you anchored in a world that no longer serves your growing light.

The light flowing in is transforming all that is dense and bringing to the surface any energy that needs to be transmuted. You are literally going through an energetic upgrade and being prepared for a more expanded state of being.

Support your body as it moves through these changes. Slow down, connect with nature, rest, drink more water and eat fresh foods. Your vibration is being raised. You are on the path of ascension. Be patient and gentle with your body during this time.

EXERCISE Slow down and rest.
Eat light-filled foods. Hydrate with clean
drinking water and ground your energy to
Mother Earth. Get sun each day and keep
electromagnetic devices to a minimum.

AFFIRMATION I lovingly and
compassionately choose to support my
body through this time of change.

STOP DOING, START BEING

STOP DOING AND START BEING THE LIGHT THAT YOU TRULY ARE.

In a world that is so fast paced it can be all too easy to get caught up in a chaotic life of doing, doing, doing. There may be feelings of being left behind when you are not keeping up with your self-imposed expectations.

Loved one, if you have drawn this card it is time to stop doing and start being. Take a deep breath and breathe out. Ask yourself: 'Are you who you are because of what you do, or does what you do reflect who you are?'

Having an abundant, joy-filled life stems from first being. This naturally moves you in the direction of doing. From doing you then go on to having. For example, if you are doing so much to generate wealth but it constantly feels like an uphill struggle, at a deeper level you are closed to prosperity.

When you open yourself up to pure beingness you are clear about being one with abundance. This deeper knowing of being one with abundance flows effortlessly in the direction of prosperity.

Stay conscious of your doing and always see if what you are doing is first coming from a place of being.

EXERCISE Take some time out to just sit in the presence of beingness.

AFFIRMATION Divinely guided, I am a magnificent being of light creating a life of choice.

32

TRUE LOVE

TO ATTRACT TRUE LOVE IS TO
FIRST EMBODY TRUE LOVE.

When you embody true love within yourself you are choosing to love yourself without judgement and criticism. You love and accept all aspects of yourself with compassion.

When you do this you emit a frequency that draws to you companions and connections in synergy with your loving vibration.

There have been many moments on your journey when you have felt despair and loneliness. Exhausted by failed relationships and shallow connections, you longed for more. Rest assured, loved one, that period is coming to an end.

Through your own internal shifts and realisations you herald in a new chapter, a chapter filled with bliss, joy, harmony, deep loving connections and lasting fulfilment.

Drink from the chalice of love. Now it is your turn to experience the wonder and magic of true love, love that is reflective of the true love that is you. Remember to fully allow others to give to you as you give to them. Do this to complete the circuit of love between giving and receiving.

Go forth and enjoy the gifts of love. So much wonder, adventure and fun await. Loved one, your wishes are coming true.

EXERCISE Look in the mirror with absolute love and say out loud: 'I am true love.'

AFFIRMATION Through unconditional love my magnificent soul is nurtured to thrive.

33

RISE ABOVE

'YOU HAVE THE POWER WITHIN YOU TO RISE ABOVE WHATEVER IS CURRENTLY SEEKING TO BRING YOU DOWN.'

– UNKNOWN

You are a divine spiritual being having this human experience through your body, but you are not this body. When your body is feeling overwhelmed, step back and observe the experience. Ask your body: 'How can I best support you through this?', then listen to the intelligence of your body through the quiet whispers of your soul.

Perhaps you may have to adjust your diet or lifestyle or even take some time out to rest. By doing this you step more into your authentic power, which then supports your body.

By staying conscious you are not falling into the illusions of the mind that tell you you are not whole. Loved one, this card reminds you that you are whole. Through this truth stay in your light and power, for the body entrains to the wholeness and balance of your mind. You are able to rise above any seemingly impossible challenge through understanding and expanded awareness.

It is only when you forget who you are and get lost in the human experience that the illusion of suffering becomes your world. Remember, loved one, you are the light.

EXERCISE Take a moment to feel your body. Feel it breathing in and out. Ask your body how it feels. Listen to the answer. Now ask yourself how you can best support your body through this time.

AFFIRMATION I rise with conscious awareness above the illusions of suffering born from the mind.

34

STAR CONSCIOUSNESS

**STARS ARE BORN TO SHINE,
SO UNLEASH THE FULL MAGNIFICENCE
AND BRILLIANCE OF YOUR RADIANT LIGHT.**

Within the consciousness of every soul are seeds of light connected to source. Conscious starseeds are those who are awake to this truth. They embody, integrate and consistently nurture this light of love within themselves.

Loved one, this card reminds you that you are energetically connected to other conscious starseeds through a web of light that spans across the galaxy. Through this network this light is amplified. This magnified energy of love is assisting humanity during this time of ascension.

Starseeded soul, your star family is scattered across the globe. By connecting to this unified field of consciousness you amplify the collective energy of love.

Although you are connected energetically to all souls, this conscious web of light operates at a different frequency, a bandwidth that attunes to the resonance of an open heart and mind aligned with the light of truth.

Use this means of frequency to tap into this energy field of interstellar light and connect to souls of the same resonance to expand and strengthen the healing power of love.

EXERCISE Visualise a light-filled star radiating out from your third eye. See this light expanding out to your entire being. Place your hands on your heart, and in your mind's eye see the earth. Allow your star family to be revealed to you through sparks of blue light scattered around the planet connected through light.

AFFIRMATION In service to the divine, I unite with kindred souls who harmonise in the resonance of love.

LIVE THE WAY

LEAD THE WAY BY LIVING THE WAY WITH UNCONDITIONAL LOVE, COMPASSION AND TRUTH.

In a world of duality there can be much suffering and pain. It is not always easy to watch those you love live within the confines and limitations of their own mind.

As hard as this may be for you, trust the process. Your loved ones are choosing paths that are best aligned for their growing souls. Unconditional love is simply holding space for these souls to make their own choices.

You best serve these souls by shining your own light fearlessly in all you do. Lead the way by first living the way. This is your best way to be of service to all those around you. In time they will be inspired by your courage and flight.

Through your compassion, unconditional love and detachment from the dualistic polarities of life you ignite a curious spark within others to look deeper into the nature of judgement, fear and defining beliefs within themselves.

Loved one, thank you! You are so appreciated. Thank you for being a beautiful reflection of cosmic consciousness, the divine creative source of love. Your light is so magnificent.

EXERCISE With no judgement, express unconditional love and compassion to all those around you despite situations, views and choices.

AFFIRMATION May the light of love within me always be a beautiful mirror to the light of truth within all.

LOVE UNBOUND

WE CAN BE BOUND BY OUR DESIRES OR FREED BY THE TOTALITY OF LOVE.

This oracle guides you to look more closely at your life. Are there any areas in which you feel limited and even bound by your own desires?

Desire can be a very seductive, lucrative form of energy that can keep your soul feeling constantly energetically hungry: hunger that's never quite fulfilled. It is so easy to stay imprisoned in a life that is void of true happiness, love and lasting fulfilment.

Spirit has heard your call to experience great love. Love in its many forms surrounds you, but it is up to you to first relinquish all that does not serve you.

If you wish to experience a more loving sacred connection, connect with yourself more deeply by unconditionally loving and accepting all facets of yourself. This includes the aspects you may wish to be freed from. This will free you from energy that keeps you bound.

Loved one, now is the time to choose. Do you wish to stay bound by your desires or freed by the totality of love?

Do not give up. Love will prevail.

EXERCISE Close your eyes and look within. Are there any areas that keep you bound? Visualise yourself talking to that aspect of self. Embrace this part of you with absolute unconditional love, compassion and acceptance.

AFFIRMATION I experience greater love by unconditionally loving and accepting all facets of myself.

ACKNOWLEDGEMENTS

A big thank you to my star family, who support and inspire me daily with their unconditional love, guidance and support.

Thank to my beautiful sister Narayne for her continued support and inspiration with the creation of this oracle.

To all my soul brothers and sisters, you know who you are. I am honoured to have you in my life.

To the source of creation, I thank you …

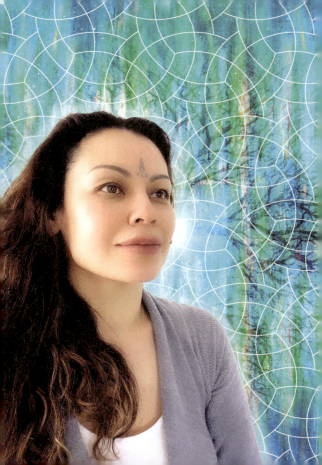

ABOUT THE
AUTHOR AND
ARTIST

As an intuitive soul guide and spirit artist, Nari Anastarsia is passionately driven to assist others remember their own unique creative light. Inspired by her own transformational journey, Nari shares her energy with the world through creative endeavours that touch and invoke the soul.

Having a deeply profound connection with Mother Earth, she expresses her light through her work as a soul guide, artist and author.

Guided by higher vibrations of love, Nari's nature is uniquely expressed through her visionary creations. It is through her creativity that she facilitates healing that touches the soul and awakens the heart. Serving as an inspirational beacon of light, Nari's creative work quietly illuminates souls from all around the world.

You can find out more and connect with Nari at:

www.narianastarsia.com
f narianastarsia
○ narianastarsia

OTHER TITLES BY NARI ANASTARSIA

COSMIC ORACLE

Activate your soul to the memory of its true creative potential with 36 visionary artworks containing daily healing messages for growth, clarity and direction.

ISBN: 9781922579683

AVATAR ORACLE

This powerful deck of 36 cards has been created to guide and support humanity through the immense changes and energy shifts occuring presently on Mother Earth.

ISBN: 9781922579720